EEO MANAGEMENT:

How to Advance Equal Opportunity without Using Quotas or Singing Kumbaya

MICHAEL WADE

DEDICATION

To those who handle an important and demanding job with thorough professionalism. By doing so, they have made a positive difference in the lives of many and in the civic health of their nation.

"A few strong instincts and a few plain rules suffice us."
Ralph Waldo Emerson

"Change before you have to."
Jack Welch

Note: The ideas and opinions given in this book are for informational purposes only and are in no way intended to be, nor should they be, a substitute for legal advice. Anyone with a legal question should consult an attorney.

[The best EEO officers know a lot of great attorneys.]

Contents

INTRODUCTION

It is not difficult to find workshops and books on Equal Employment Opportunity, Affirmative Action, and Diversity. "Diversity" in particular has become such a hot ticket that many EEO and Affirmative Action programs are called "diversity" programs when in fact the responsibilities are quite different.

What is difficult, however, is to find guidance on how to manage such programs. This book was written to fill that gap.

I briefly toyed with the idea of using "Guidance from a Curmudgeon" as the title because over the years I've often differed with people in the field, especially those who favor multiculturalism over assimilation and who inadvertently contribute to a culture of victimhood. I'll take my shots as we progress, but the main thrust of this book will be to give program managers the street smarts they need to navigate one of the trickiest and most unforgiving jobs in the workplace.

As a nation, we have gone a long way from the days of my childhood, when a visit to the segregated South exposed me to Whites Only drinking fountains and lunch counters. Often, there seems to be a reluctance to acknowledge progress, as if doing so would trigger complacency and backsliding. Failing to do so, however, fosters demoralization. Even worse, it is a distortion of reality.

The very idea of equal opportunity runs throughout American history. We see it in the words and arguments of the nation's founders, watch as it bleeds during the Civil War, and hear it sung and proclaimed during the civil rights movement.

News articles often tell of revolutionaries around the world. They get it wrong. We Americans are the true revolutionaries. There is no other nation on Earth that gives as much attention or protection to the rights of the individual as does the United States of America. Whether that continuing American Revolution succeeds will depend in part on the ability of people to enjoy equal opportunity in the workplace. That, in turn, will depend upon how well EEO programs are managed.

Regardless of your job title, you can play a key role.

Michael Wade
Phoenix, 2011

A QUICK WORD ON TERMINOLOGY

In order to avoid the rather lengthy EEO/AA/DM abbreviation, I'll simply use EEO to refer to all three programs when discussing them in general and will give specific names when addressing them individually. I also use "EEO Officer" as the title of the head of the EEO function.

WHAT "THEY" THINK OF YOU

"Every organization has a Siberia."
– Warren Bennis

The Bad News is that EEO offices are often viewed negatively. In over 30 years of advising organizations on EEO management, I've heard them described as "dumping grounds;" "hall closet specialties," and "the end of the line."

There is a reason for those cruel labels:

In many cases, they're true.

Ouch. That's not pleasant. It would be much more pleasing to write that the EEO function is usually a highly regarded and valued member of the top management team, but you and I know that usually is not the case. If we are going to explore how to manage such programs it is important to have a clear view of the obstacles. Image is one of them. Many EEO operations are not staffed by the cream of the crop. They often get a mixture of zealots, mavericks, idealists, and bureaucrats. The subject itself is a specialty and many organizations don't have a career ladder that takes people beyond the top EEO job. As a result, the best and the brightest do not flock to the field. Why do so when you'll be stigmatized and blocked from promotions?

There are bright and dedicated people in the EEO subject area but – like honest lawyers – they have to toil to counter negative images. Let one fanatic turn a diversity workshop into a re-education camp and you'll be cleaning up the mess for years.

The Good News is it doesn't have to be that way. Excellent EEO professionals have built credible and highly effective programs. They've fended off the negative aspects of the profession and have established systems that multiply support for equal opportunity in even the unlikeliest of quarters.

In the following pages, we'll examine how that is done.

AN OPERATING PHILOSOPHY

"It is a characteristic mistake of the enlightened to demand too much of humans and then to loathe them for falling short."
- Michael Novak

Trust is the foundation of good management. Being trustworthy does not only mean that you are honest and that you do what you say you will do, it also means that you are competent. You may be the most honest and caring person in the world, but if you cannot produce the goods, you are unreliable. All of the elements of effectiveness – knowledge, judgment, and execution - fall under the umbrella of trust.

Your goal as an EEO manager is to build a climate of trust in your organization. If people trust management, they won't sue it. If they trust their supervisors, they won't file complaints against them. When you strip away the layers of an employee relations or EEO complaint, at its core you will find a lack of trust.

What does this mean in terms of your daily practices?

It means that doing right is more important than being right. Let me give an example. Years ago, when I was the EEO Administrator for the City of Phoenix, Arizona, employees would, on occasion, threaten to sue us. My response was simple: "Go right ahead. If we are wrong, we should be corrected." When people filed internal complaints with our office, we gave them a sheet with the addresses and phone numbers of the federal and state enforcement agencies where they could also file.

You can imagine the reaction of some department heads when they learned of that practice. "What are you doing? Why are you telling them that they can file complaints with the Equal Employment Opportunity Commission and with the Attorney General's Office?" The answer was simple: We were building credibility. We were letting them know that we were not afraid of complaints and we were giving them the information needed to make an informed decision.

Consider this: If we took the view that the organization must be protected at all costs and that we should try to squelch complaints, that would be the equivalent of slapping a bandage on a potential cancer. The EEO office has a responsibility to prevent and remove illegal discrimination from the workplace. At times, that involves admitting that the organization has screwed up and that corrective action must be taken.

Your role is not to serve as a paralegal for management. When persuasive evidence of illegal discrimination is present, your job is to get management to face up to the truth. When bad management practices come close to, but do not cross the line into, illegal discrimination, you need to get those practices changed. This requires two things:

1. You have to be persuasive; and
2. You have to be honest.

Start with the second one. If you cannot be honest in the job, if you get bullied or seduced into covering up discrimination, then you need to get out of that job. You are worse than worthless because your presence implies that the organization's position has merit. You are an accessory to a managerial fraud. Don't participate. Get the hell out of there.

The need to be persuasive will be discussed at length later. I'll just note for now that a major sin of some EEO professionals is not fighting the right battles. They jump on some good old boy for a minor league sexist comment when that person has a good heart and is a potential ally. You build coalitions through addition, not subtraction. Creating a climate of trust requires that corrective actions not be disproportionate.

Knowing that you do not have to carry water for discriminatory management simplifies the world enormously. You won't lose sleep trying to figure out how to defend the indefensible.

But that brings up another key point: You'll need to set a higher standard than mere legal compliance. I hear executives and managers say, "We obey the law." Oh wow, that's impressive. You obey the law?

Legal compliance is the *lowest* standard. If you are going to prevent discrimination, you need to get management to adopt a higher one. Think of legal compliance as a series of thickets or hedges. If all you do is aim for legal compliance, you'll be caught in the thickets. You'll be at the mercy of every gray court case out there and there are plenty of them.

You want to set a higher standard that doesn't even come close to a legal violation. That is why asking if an action is legal is just a part of the process. There are many things that are legal that are also - as a Southern friend of mine puts it - "mean and hateful."

There is another philosophical point to keep in mind. You are the advocate for equal opportunity. You are not the advocate for women, minorities, gays, people with disabilities, old people, young people, religious people, agnostics, white guys, fat people, or whatever possible victim status is alleged. You are not in charge of the equal results program. You strive for a nondiscriminatory environment in which, to the greatest degree possible, people are selected, evaluated, and promoted on their abilities. [I once saw a company that put in its ads, "We discriminate solely on the basis of merit."]

Equal opportunity means people also have the opportunity to fail. That may be a shock in a world where children's teams hand out trophies for warming the bench, but a big part of life's ground rules involves failing. Believe me. I've been there. Several times in fact. Failure is not fun, but it is very instructive.

So you're sort of in the Tough Love business. You know that not everyone out there can pull himself up by his bootstraps, but you also know that constantly telling people that they're victims is a sure way of keeping them down. [Not many football coaches boost performance by telling their players that the game is rigged for the other side.] Moreover, equal opportunity is the law. Preferential treatment isn't. [One of the conflicting habits of some Affirmative Action professionals is to deny that Affirmative Action involves hiring quotas and then, in almost the next breath, declare that eliminating quotas will damage Affirmative Action. It's quite a trick.]

If sorting out equal opportunity from equal result isn't hard enough, EEO professionals are further tempted off the track when they are given Affirmative Action and Diversity Management responsibilities. Those two sidekicks have separate agendas and the maps they carry don't quite match. If you are going to succeed, it needs to be made clear just who is in charge.

And yes, one is more equal than the others.

EEO'S SKEPTICS

"Every problem has a gift for you in its hands."
- Richard Bach

First, let's take a quick detour to consider how managers and supervisors are informally educated in EEO. They read the same general news sources you do and probably give stories about EEO the same rapt attention that you pay to stories about engineering or street-cleaning. As a result, they quite reasonably slap on a convenient label containing a paragraph of generalizations on the subject. Those generalizations remain until something causes them to be altered.

For many, the generalizations are that white males are not protected by civil rights laws; all Affirmative Action involves preferences; discrimination cases are easy to win; plaintiffs are only trying to game the system; merit and job standards are about to expire; and there is no business reason for EEO and Affirmative Action other than keeping the government off of your back.

For others – especially those who are victims of Sociology courses - the generalizations are that discrimination is rampant; women are always paid less than men; Affirmative Action never uses quotas; people who are powerless cannot be racist; plaintiffs are noble; employers are evil; there is no such thing as "best qualified"; merit systems are inherently slanted against minorities; and the government civil rights enforcement agencies seldom overreach.

When you walk into a department to discuss EEO and its related topics, recognize that a number of the people in the room will hold attitudes from these two groups. Those who believe you are doing too much may be seated right next to those who believe you are doing too little.

You can make up your own mind as to which side is closest to the truth but you'd better be able to address their arguments. If you fail to do so, they'll write you off as just another Tool of The Powers That Be and your ability to persuade will be gone.

Remember: EEO management is not difficult unless you want to do it well.

WHEN UPPER MANAGEMENT IS WIMPY

"If you have always believed that everyone should play by the same rules and be judged by the same standards, that would have gotten you labeled a radical 60 years ago, a liberal 30 years ago and a racist today."
– Thomas Sowell

Pretend that two consulting firms are being considered by upper management for a training project related to diversity.

Firm X is noted for its beliefs that women, minorities, and other groups are oppressed in the workplace by pervasive racism, sexism, and other sins. Its classes focus on re-educating the workforce so employees and managers embrace multiculturalism. It disdains the concept of color-blindness as unrealistic, outdated, and even dangerous.

Firm Y favors assimilation and a strong policy of nondiscrimination. It opposes quotas and stresses opportunity over result. Its programs emphasize the importance of unity and it avoids labeling.

Which firm will get the deal?

Unfortunately, in many cases the first firm will be chosen. Why? Because a masochistic upper management may decide that it can distance itself from any guilt by hiring the guilt-mongers. In this bold new world, they would pick Eldridge Cleaver or Malcolm X over Martin Luther King Jr.

I have a word for such wimpy management: Contemptible.

Upper managers who encourage divisiveness in the names of equal opportunity and diversity are doing no one a favor except for the race-baiting consultants who walk away with a hefty pay check.

By catering to such theories, they harm assimilation and opportunity. They foster large pockets of resistance within the workplace.

If you sense that you might be dealing with an upper management team that would fall into that trap, you need to make a special effort to brief them on the core philosophy of EEO and on why the guilt-inducing programs are harmful. Don't assume that they will be able to spot the problems on their own. Many otherwise hard-nosed executives may fall prey to the siren songs of the social engineers. You need to keep them on the right track.

EEO/AA/DM

*"The hard stuff is easy.
The soft stuff is hard.
And the soft stuff is
a lot more important
than the hard stuff."*
- Milliken & Company

Back to terminology. Here it is in a nutshell:

Equal Employment Opportunity (EEO) means Thou Shalt Not Discriminate on the basis of race, sex, national origin, color, religion, age, disability, and – in some jurisdictions and probably soon on the federal level – sexual orientation. Note: This does not require that employers behave fairly or logically. Nay, the EEO standard is much lower. It requires nondiscrimination. You may not realize it, but that is very good news. It is far easier to determine whether or not there was illegal discrimination than to decide just what is "fair." [Parents can attest to this.] As for being illogical, let us ignore that morass other than to mention that if management had to throw out illogical decisions, on some days that could shut down the entire operation.

Affirmative Action means that the employer will go beyond a policy of nondiscrimination to ensure that people who may have been excluded in the past are given a chance to compete. You don't open your door at 2 a.m. and whisper, "We're hiring women and minorities." You have open recruitment. You send out notices. You make sure that your selection process is nondiscriminatory and then – this is a very important "and then" – you hire the best qualified person for the job. Period.

That is Good Affirmative Action. Unfortunately, Good Affirmative Action has an evil twin, Bad Affirmative Action. That creature uses quotas. It eludes merit standards and does not select the best qualified person for the job. It violates EEO.

You're heard of "reverse discrimination?" There's no such thing as reverse discrimination. It's discrimination.

When the 1964 Civil Rights Bill was being debated in the United States Senate, Senator Hubert H. Humphrey declared that nothing in the bill required preferences. He vowed to eat the bill if it did. Unfortunately, many employers slipped away from that interpretation. They caved in to shake-down artists and interest groups who sought preferences. By doing so, they have seriously harmed the cause of civil rights. How? Because the strict application of the principle of equal opportunity is an essential component of any EEO program. Drift away from it, adopt a wink-wink-nudge-nudge attitude that hides quotas behind "goals" and does not select the best qualified, and you and the program will no longer be trustworthy.

Diversity Management is the newcomer to the dance. Organizations enforced EEO and became nondiscriminatory, they used Affirmative Action and recruited a more diverse workforce, and then they realized that if they were going to retain and supervise that diverse pool of workers, they needed to know how to manage differences.

Like Affirmative Action, Diversity Management has a good and bad side. The Good Diversity Management analyzes the preferences and needs of various groups in order to make sure they aren't ignored with some one size-fits-all policy or practice that makes no sense. It also teaches managers, supervisors, and employees about diverse communication styles. In essence, it focuses on good management skills.

The Bad Diversity Management is politically correct. It drifts into lengthy workshop discussions of racism, sexism, homophobia, etc. and divides more than it unites. [Such discussions are not inherently harmful if: (1) they are conducted by well-qualified professionals; (2) the emphasis is more on commonality than on differences; and (3) enough time is devoted to bring the group back together. Most organizations lack the resources and time to do so.]

Diversity Management stresses paying attention to differences. This confuses many employees as they understandably see a conflict with EEO. "Wait a minute," they say. "EEO tells us to be color-blind and Diversity Management tells us to be color-conscious. What gives?" The answer is that EEO bars *adverse* treatment that is based on one of the illegal categories. It does not bar positive treatment that does not harm anyone. Example: I am meeting with an employee who is from an ethnic group that tends to discuss non-business subjects before easing into the business topic. If I follow that conversation pattern, I may have treated that employee differently than I would have treated a person from another group, but I have not harmed anyone. There is no conflict with EEO.

When can Diversity Management conflict with EEO? If quotas are used to achieve diversity, that may violate EEO. If whites are stigmatized as racists, that may violate EEO.

Here is a simple ground rule: If Affirmative Action or Diversity Management conflict with EEO, EEO wins. It has a far firmer grounding in statutory and case law and it has the added advantage of being managerially sound. Far more people in the workplace will, without hesitation, back EEO than will support Affirmative Action or Diversity Management. It is the cornerstone of your program.

Which brings us to some key concepts that are applied to discrimination cases.

Disparate Treatment cases are the ones people normally think of when they think of discrimination. X treats Y adversely because of Y's race, sex, national origin, color, religion, age, disability or sexual orientation. Not enjoyable cases to deal with but they are fairly straightforward. If the evidence shows that there is reasonable cause (i.e., it was more likely than not) that illegal discrimination was the reason for the adverse treatment, X wins. We will take Y out and hurt and punish him or her for that behavior. Perhaps we'll even terminate Y.

Disparate Impact (sometimes known as Adverse Impact) is a very different animal. It is applied in cases where a policy, practice, standard, or requirement is neutrally applied but adversely affects a group. The burden then shifts to the employer to justify the policy, practice, standard or requirement.

If the employer can pass that test, it doesn't matter how many people are excluded. The policy, practice, standard or requirement will stand. If the employer cannot pass that test, the employer loses.

Plaintiff attorneys love disparate impact because those cases involve large numbers of people and readily available documentation, such as pass/fail rates and whether tests have been validated. [Incidentally, don't take the "this test has been validated" claims of professional testing services on face value. You don't want to learn in a courtroom that the study was superficial and limited in scope.]

What this means is that you and your associates must learn how to think like a plaintiff attorney. Make that a junk-yard dog plaintiff attorney. You need to war-game your organization's recruitment and selection procedures. You need to question education and experience requirements and determine which ones are truly necessary. You need to insert weasel words, such as "Training and Experience May Be Substituted for Education" in job descriptions and recruitment announcements.

In other words, challenge your own standards and practices before someone else does. To borrow a great line from Jack Welch: "Change before you have to."

You'll be amazed at what crawls out. You'll find departments that can't provide a plausible explanation for various requirements. They've required certain items or credentials because they always required them. They can't explain why they demand five years of experience as opposed to four or three or seven. They may not enjoy this exercise – in fact, count on that – but it is better for them to be challenged by you than by someone who will try to make them out to be Bull Connor.

The law makes a big shift when the subject moves from traditional areas of discrimination (think race, sex, national origin) and enters the realm of disability. Before, the emphasis has been on equal treatment and now, in order to avoid discrimination, you have to engage in different treatment. To add to the confusion, money is often involved.

It is easy to understand why these seem like mixed signals, because they are. With disability discrimination, managers and supervisors need to learn about reasonable accommodation, determining the essential functions of the job, and undue hardship. This isn't that complicated but it is different, especially if you don't spend weekends grooving over the latest accommodation cases instead of watching football, jogging or going to the movies.

Remember, the information sources for many of your managers and supervisors are telling them that the courts are giving away the store. When they hear someone talk about providing "reasonable accommodation" for disabled employees and applicants, they may be inclined to block out the "reasonable" part and think of *unlimited accommodation*. That's why it is important to stress "reasonable."

The goal in disability accommodation cases is to render the disability irrelevant. You want to provide reasonable accommodation so the disability becomes a non-issue:

Equipment accessible? Check.
Work area accessible? Check.
Restrooms accessible? Check.
Parking and building accessible? Check.

Great, now the person can be judged on how well he or she performs the job. The disability is not mentioned because it is as relevant as their aunt in Cleveland. If the employee does well, there should be rewards. If not, coaching and counseling and perhaps even discipline should be used.

And that brings up an important point. People with disabilities are people. They don't have a special edge in terms of nobility. Although most people with disabilities are fine folks, as with any large group their ranks also include the same type of manipulators you may find with non-disabled people.

—

Fortunately, if you handle reasonable accommodation in a professional manner, you'll thwart many of the manipulators. How is that done? Manipulators want to make demands and then watch as you cave in. They don't want medical opinions and experts. I've found that many of them back off when they learn that the employer is willing to get a professional analysis of their requests. The beauty of that, of course, is that if the person is not manipulating or playing games, you've still handled the matter in the proper manner.

By the way, a selling point when discussing disability accommodation issues is the potentially large scope of the covered group. As one disability rights attorney put it, "I don't think of myself as disabled. I think of the rest of you as temporarily able-bodied." Somewhat macabre perhaps, but he's probably correct. If you're not disabled now, give yourself time.

The Americans with Disabilities Act Amendments Act has tilted the scales in favor of plaintiffs. Whereas before there was considerable attention given to whether the plaintiff fit the definition of disabled and whether there was substantial limitation, now the Equal Employment Opportunity Commission will rush past that and focus on whether there was discrimination. As with any of these questions, consult with your attorney. Don't delay.

The reasonable accommodation versus undue hardship test is also applied to religious discrimination in the workplace. It is easier, however, to show undue hardship in the accommodation of religious beliefs and practices if only because all of us – including atheists and agnostics – may be protected in the religious discrimination prohibition. Accommodating one person may involve violating the rights of another. Since rendering yourself vulnerable to liability can be regarded as undue hardship, the large pool of other potential complainants can trigger the undue hardship argument. It will be interesting to see if the expansive coverage of the ADA Amendments Act creates similar potential conflicts in disability cases.

GAINING CLOUT AND COMPETENCE

"You know what I really need?
A badge. A stinking badge."
- Norm MacDonald

A management rule is that organizations get the results they are designed to get. It will be very difficult to have a successful EEO program if the design is flawed. Here are some recommendations:

Don't Report to HR. One of the biggest mistakes that organizations make is tucking the EEO function within the Human Resources Department. The rationale seems to be that HR deals with people issues and EEO does the same, so let's put them together. That decision might make sense with smaller employers in which HR becomes a jack of all trades and where the HR Director may double as the EEO Officer, but with larger employers it is a huge mistake.

The reason is simple: EEO needs to be able to investigate Human Resources. HR handles recruitment and selection, signs off on major discipline, administers exams, and makes accommodation decisions. All of those activities attract discrimination allegations. If the organization is going to have a credible internal complaint process, it helps if the EEO Officer is beyond the direct influence of the HR Director. This doesn't mean that they can't work well together and that they won't have an amiable relationship, but as Robert Frost reminded us, "Good fences make good neighbors." The relationship between EEO and HR is one of those areas where a clear boundary helps.

If this doesn't seem feasible in your organization, there are some options. One compromise is used in the American military's equal opportunity programs where the unit Equal Opportunity Officer may report to HR but also is guaranteed, by regulation, direct access to the commanding officer. Another is to have the EEO function as part of the Law Department, but with direct access to the CEO.

It is possible to place EEO, Affirmative Action, and Diversity Management into separate areas, with EEO being completely separate or in the Law Department, and Affirmative Action and Diversity Management being in the HR Department. That would give EEO the independence needed for discrimination investigations while preventing the possible conflict that may arise when EEO and Affirmative Action are responsibilities of the same office. Affirmative Action efforts, like other HR-related functions, have the potential to generate discrimination cases.

Ideally, the EEO Office should be a separate function with direct access to the Chief Executive Officer, but you have to deal with the possible organization, not the ideal one. Having direct access to the top decision maker increases the likelihood of objectivity and clout.

Job Titles. A quick word: Are you an EEO Director, Administrator, Manager, Officer, Coordinator, Analyst, Consultant, Advisor or Specialist? Whatever the title, it will either add or detract from your clout. If you get stuck with a less than desirable title, don't despair. Real clout can be achieved through your performance.

I'll use the title of EEO Officer in this book simply because it is more generic.

EEO Staff Responsibilities. As for your staff, you'll probably have some secretarial staff and then a team of specialists to deal with investigations, Affirmative Action, and diversity issues. Don't compromise on quality when filling these positions. If you can't find or afford the right person, outsource the job.

Expect that over time, the specialists will become territorial. I once experimented with periodically rotating the responsibilities of a group of specialists. I thought the idea had merit since it would give them greater breadth of experience and would strengthen the office as a whole.

They hated it. They liked their comfort zones and who can blame them? After a few months, I scrapped the idea and they went back to their original responsibilities. The one benefit was they gained a better appreciation of what the other people had to handle. They learned that co-workers who may have seemed to be goofing off actually had a pretty serious workload.

EEO Officer Responsibilities. Management scholar Henry Mintzberg wrote that all managers have these responsibilities: Figurehead, Leader, Liaison, Monitor, Disseminator, Spokesperson, Entrepreneur, Disturbance Handler, Resource Allocator, and Negotiator.

Adapting Mintzberg's groupings, the EEO Officer responsibilities can be broken down as follows:

—

Bias Cop: You prevent discrimination; monitor the work environment and personnel practices; audit to ensure compliance with laws and regulations; handle discrimination complaints; deal with outside enforcement agencies and with litigation; and train executives, managers, and employees.

Recruiter: You prepare and update the Affirmative Action Program; disseminate the EEO/Affirmative Action Policy; implement targeted recruiting practices; report to management on goals and progress; handle disabled and veterans issues; and train executives, managers, and employees on recruitment and selection issues.

Community Liaison: You serve as a spokesperson and establish ties to community groups.

Change Agent: You negotiate, schmooze; reconcile EEO, Affirmative Action, and Diversity Management; change behavior within the organization; and change your role as the organization itself changes.

Often, the job seems to be divided into two jobs: Consultant and Cop. As much as possible, you want to operate in the Consultant capacity so you'll have to spend less time being a Cop.

Many organizations blunder by following an informal quota system in selecting the EEO Officer. It may seem politically savvy to reserve that slot for a Black or a Hispanic or a woman, but the EEO job – like all of your other positions – should be filled by the best qualified candidate. If you play the quota game in filling that position, it will be hard to convince people that you are above that game when filling other positions. Furthermore, you don't want the EEO Office to be viewed as an entity that is for everyone but straight white guys. Make life simple. Choose the best applicant.

Competence includes objectivity. Everyone in the EEO Office must be beyond reproach when it comes to prejudice. Skeptics will expect the EEO professionals to stack the deck in favor of minorities, women, and other groups. Such behavior cannot be tolerated. The EEO professionals must operate with a monk-like detachment and commitment to nondiscrimination. They cannot afford to become informal advocates for various groups. Their mantra must be "Equal Opportunity for All."

If someone cannot meet that standard, then the person must go. One intemperate remark on the part of an EEO professional can destroy credibility.

An unpleasant but seldom addressed topic should be acknowledged. Various interest groups often mistakenly regard the EEO Office as their turf and seek to exclude members of other groups from directing that office or holding most of the staff positions. It is not unusual to see wary looks from black groups if a Hispanic candidate is selected to direct the EEO operations and similar looks from Hispanic groups if a black is chosen. The same problem arises if a member of any other group is chosen.

As a white male, I had to overcome a series of obstacles to be selected as the EEO Officer for a major American city. [I grew to be amused at the attitudes. Some new visitors to the office would give a slight glance over my shoulder when shaking my hand as if waiting for the "real" EEO Officer to appear.] There were even times when I sensed that some of the black and Hispanic advocacy groups actually preferred having me in the post because it meant "the other side" was excluded.

This attitude is mindless and should not be encouraged by upper management in an effort to score points in the community. It is unethical and discriminatory to use an informal quota to fill any EEO position even if it is for political purposes. When upper management does that, it is gutless and unworthy of respect. It is also saying that it does not take the position seriously.

Because of common stereotypes and prejudices, EEO Offices are judged according to a very severe standard. The Engineering and the Marketing departments may blunder without having their core competence questioned. A trip-up by the EEO folks, however, will cause eyebrows to raise and people to regard it as an indication of ineptitude.

They – the skeptics out there - expect you to fail. They expect you to be unprofessional. You must change those expectations.

Confidentiality. Confidentiality of what is said in the office with regard to complaints, departments, and other workplace matters must be firmly maintained. Information should be given on a "need to know" basis. Make it very clear to your staff that there should be no luncheon discussions of sensitive subjects. Employees will not confide in your office if they feel their words will be broadcast.

Prevent Factions. Many EEO offices inadvertently create factions. The EEO people, the Affirmative Action people, and the Diversity Management people form different circles while the office administrative staff members shake their heads at all three groups. I strongly recommend that you establish this simple ground rule: If anyone has a problem with a co-worker, they will discuss the problem with the co-worker. [This does not apply to complaints such as "Clyde slipped his hand up my skirt" or "Mary has a gun in her desk and thinks we're Martians."]

If the problem cannot be resolved with the co-worker, then the two of them need to come to you. What this policy prevents is the common scenario in which one or each of the disputing employees comes to you without having confronted their co-worker and expects you to shape up their peer. That is a trap. Don't step into it. That "behind the scenes" strategy erodes trust and it will gobble up sizable chunks of your time.

Factions may also form on other grounds. You may find Minorities versus White Women or Hispanics versus Blacks or Young versus Old. Squelch those divisions by stressing openness and trustworthiness. At the heart of conflict is a lack of trust. That lack may be nurtured by outright bias or by the suspicion that one side or the other is being favored. You cannot permit that to continue or you'll soon have a dysfunctional office. You'd get more done with a staff of two who work together well than with a staff of two hundred who are back-biting and back-stabbing.

Physical Security. There will be times when you and your employees may encounter very angry people or individuals who are emotionally disturbed. You should seriously consider the use of a subtle warning system, some neutral phrase that might signal a warning to a co-worker or perhaps even a hidden buzzer system that will let your secretary know that you need an excuse to end a meeting. Our office had a button under the edge of my desk. If I pressed it, the secretary in the front office would knock on my door and announce that my boss wanted to see me immediately in his office. The button was there for years and I never used it, but there were a few occasions when it was reassuring to know that the option was available.

Naturally, if there is evidence that more stringent security measures are needed, you should take them. There are violence prevention experts who can provide specific guidance.

BUILD A PRESENCE

"Sometimes I get the feeling that the whole world is
against me, but deep down I know that's not true.
Some of the smaller countries are neutral."
- Robert Orben

The world is often very superficial. If your appearance
signals that you are a low-ranking, powerless person,
you'll be treated accordingly.

Look and Sound Ultra-Professional. Dress and
speak like a serious professional. Don't make threats
or brag. Do your homework. Understate your case.
Coordinate your proposals so you don't get blindsided.
Err on the side of being boringly competent.

Have an Appropriate Office Location. The EEO
Office should be in a location that denotes status and
not exile. The décor should be utilitarian and tasteful.
The location should permit employees who might have
complaints to slip through the door without being
spotted by others. [For example, having an EEO
Office at the back of the Human Resources
Department would be a poor choice because
employees would have to walk the gauntlet of scrutiny
before reaching the EEO Office's door.]

Privacy is crucial. If this seems a little paranoid, consider the trepidation that may be carried by an employee with a complaint. In my EEO Officer days, I found that if I said hello to someone in an elevator, that person's associates might turn and ask the individual, "How did you meet him?" The implication was that the person must have been involved in an investigation.

Clearly, a collection of open office cubicles would not be appropriate for an EEO function. You need private offices with thick walls.

Get Access to a Good Employment Attorney. On second thought, make that "to a GREAT employment attorney." Upper management may groan about the legal fees, but the costs will be modest compared to what will be paid if discrimination problems are not prevented. Your in-house counsel may have the experience to handle such matters, but that is usually not the case. You want advice from someone who lives and breathes EEO. You'll find that those ten minute telephone conversations to run decisions by the experienced EEO attorney will be a bargain in the long run.

Some quick tips on dealing with your employment attorney:

Get a person who has specific and substantive experience, but also make sure that you have compatible personalities. You will need to be able to get on the same wave length and if your personalities don't click, that will be a problem.

Don't tell them fairy tales. Have a relationship of absolute candor. Tell them the facts and bring them up to speed on any office politics-related traps that might pose problems. Conversely, make it very clear that they are not to drop you on your head.

Don't get someone who wants to take everything to the U.S. Supreme Court but also don't have a lawyer who is afraid to go to court. [Not every employment attorney has courtroom experience.]

Require the use of plain language and don't let them always say "No." Lawyers are trained to be risk-adverse. They are natural worriers who can cough up three worst case scenarios before breakfast and not miss a sip of coffee. For lawyers, the status quo is usually legally defensible and making changes involves risk. Did I mention they don't like risk? That's why you need to give them the context and explain why it is intolerable. I recall an employment attorney who suggested frequent use of the phrase, "We can't live with this" whenever discussing a potential termination case with an attorney. He noted that if you don't bring that to their attention, lawyers will assume that you can live with it; perhaps even with a smile on your face. (Lawyer: "So this Charles Manson character that you want to terminate has just a few more years until retirement. Why not let him coast?")

Shun the Cosmetic. It is not very impressive to have an Ethnic Food Day when your organization is losing discrimination cases and the hiring practices are highly questionable. All that means is that the grumbling of demoralized employees may take place over plates of enchiladas and fried rice.

Many EEO Offices make the mistake of leaping to adopt flashy diversity programs before their anti-discrimination house is in order. Here's a basic strategy:

1. Get the EEO anti-discrimination efforts in place and smoothly functioning.

44

2. Review and improve your Affirmative Action outreach efforts.
3. Then, and only then, examine how diversity management efforts to retain and better manage a diverse workforce can be established.

If you jump to Step 3 before the other two Steps are firmly in place, your credibility will suffer. To use that old Texas expression, you'll be "All hat and no cattle."

Establish Your Office's Core Values. The key values are simple: We will strive to eliminate and prevent illegal discrimination. We will not use discrimination to get rid of discrimination. We will work to find, develop, and retain the best employees.

All else, as they say, is commentary.

Schmooze. You need to build your networks. Schedule individual appointments to have coffee with the department heads. Let them see you when you're not bringing bad news. Get to know their concerns and their direct reports. Listen carefully for any fears they may have about your program. Give them your home phone number so they can call you at any time. Act like an ally rather than an adversary.

This does not mean that you are going to turn into a Good Ole Boy or Gal. It should always be clear that your office won't hesitate to find against their department if they have acted improperly. The time spent with them, however, will help to prevent discrimination problems as, over time, they will feel comfortable visiting with or calling you and seeking your counsel.

Amid all of your networking with department heads, don't forget to talk to employees at all levels. When you have those conversations, do more listening than talking.

Have Significant Action Reports. Each of your direct reports should give you a written Significant Action Report every month. That report should be no longer than two pages and it should contain brief descriptions of what they regard as significant actions. If they leave out something that you regard as significant, have them revise the report and put in the needed information. Likewise, you should send your boss a monthly Significant Action Report. It lets you designate what you regard as significant and it smokes out the boss's feelings on what is or is not significant and, of course, it provides information.

Keep Your Boss Briefed. Never let your boss be embarrassed by a lack of information that you should have reported. This is especially true of bad news. You might be able to delay a bit on reporting good news but you'd better report bad news pronto. Don't dress it up. Give it straight and with a clear indication of what is known, what is not known, and what should be done in the immediate future.

Have an EEO Liaison in Each Department. Ask each department director to designate an EEO Liaison for his or her department. That person will be your contact person when you need to look at department files, schedule interviews with department witnesses, get department Affirmative Action information, and conduct training for the department. I recommend giving special training and recognition to the department liaisons.[Some "brown bag" specials; i.e., training sessions over lunch, can be very helpful.] Get to know each of your liaisons. They are your eyes and ears in the departments and can be a great source of information.

KNOW YOUR PRIORITIES

"You can't have everything.
Where would you put it?"
-   Steven Wright

Seek to Change Behavior, Not Attitudes. Here's a dirty little secret. You don't care if any of the people in your organization are closet bigots if they behave properly on the job. Lord knows we all have strange attitudes that, like vampires, might not stand the light of day. So what? If we behave properly, our employer should have no objection.

If you try to change attitudes, you will drive right into a brick wall. People will justifiably raise invasion of privacy objections and even your allies will wonder what you are doing. Resistance will intensify.

Seek instead to change behavior. It is not unusual to discover that once the behavior is changed, the attitudes are subsequently altered. Look at the polling of racial attitudes prior to the passage of the 1964 Civil Rights Act. You'll find large numbers of whites expressing objections to practices, such as sitting next to a black at a lunch counter, which would not spark any concern today. Changes in behavior produce changes in attitude.

"Pick battles big enough to matter,
small enough to win."
- Jonathon Kozol

—

Pick Your Battles. Here's a scenario: You are meeting with a department head about some job standards that you think might produce disparate impact. He tells you a story that is borderline inappropriate but which might cause the local representatives of the National Organization for Women to launch a demonstration. You know that if you stiffen and object to the humor, your chances of getting him to agree to change the job standards will evaporate. My advice is to avoid making a big deal about the joke (You might use a gentle reproach: "If you keep telling jokes like that, I'm going to have to put some leeches on you") and focus on the job standards. The standards are far more important unless the joke is deeply offensive.

You may also find that the department head, despite his occasional lapse into vaudeville routines, is a valuable ally in achieving genuine equal opportunity. Why turn him into an enemy?

The tendency of some people to call everything racist, sexist or homophobic has removed the stigma from those terms. You are after the big game; not some minor transgression.

Beware of Mission Creep. This is especially a problem in the public sector where politicians like to create committees to placate interest groups. Danger! If your office is required to staff those groups, every time it gets that dubious distinction your budget has been indirectly cut.

Another danger is that the focus of your office may become blurred. I've seen EEO offices that receive so many responsibilities that they are transformed into more of a social service agency. Let someone else take on those responsibilities.

Know the Value and Limitations of Community Groups. Community groups can assist in getting the word out to various parts of your recruitment area. They can assist in marketing. They can provide people for appointment to committees.

There is, however, one thing you do not want them to do: Run your EEO program. They not only lack the expertise, they also have a different agenda. If this fear seems groundless, keep in mind that I've encountered one major employer that let people from community groups play an advisory role in the investigation of discrimination complaints. I have no idea what management was smoking on the day that decision was made.

Another thing to keep in mind: Just because a group calls itself a civil rights group doesn't mean that it has any serious interest in equal opportunity for groups outside of its membership. Many a shake-down artist has carved out a lucrative living in the name of civil rights. Beware of groups that cloak themselves as victims but which are truly predatory.

Educate Upper Management. The executives are your Achilles' heel. They are more prone to cave in to community pressure and are often less trained in EEO matters than many first-line supervisors and far less than middle managers. Make sure that they are briefed on the big picture and that they understand the philosophy of the EEO program. Executives may favor peace over justice; a bias that is not helpful when you are battling community groups that seek special privileges.

Understand the Clout Calculations. Here's how the power arithmetic probably works in your organization:

EEO Officer vs. Department Head = Odds favor the Department Head.

EEO Officer + Lawyer vs. Department Head = Odds slightly favor the EEO Officer.

EEO Officer + Lawyer + HR Director vs. Department Head = Odds strongly favor EEO Officer.

EEO Officer + Lawyer + HR Director + CEO vs. Department Head = Department Head is a cooked goose.

Know When to Take Things Upstairs. Try as you might to seek reasonable solutions, you may encounter a department head that is thoroughly uncooperative. If the two of you cannot reach a resolution, then it is time to kick the problem upstairs. Before it reaches that point, however, check to know that the HR Director and your organization's attorney are in your corner. When all of you sit down with the CEO, you want your opponent to be the unreasonable one.

Make sure that you have objectively stated the facts, your position is reasonable, and your allies are willing to speak up. Remember: Epitomize professionalism.

AFFIRMATIVE ACTION STRATEGIES

"Plans aren't important, planning is."
-   Dwight Eisenhower

All of us know the controversy that has surrounded
Affirmative Action. Putting together an effective
Affirmative Action program is, when done properly,
the equivalent of extending the reach of your EEO
program. After all, if you want to hire the best, you
want to find the best.

Don't Condescend. Make sure that all of your
employment standards are defensible. Don't lower
them for women and minorities. As well-intended as
those efforts might be, they are condescending and
probably violate EEO.

Keep the Numbers. People may think that employers
keep statistics on race, sex, and national origin solely
for Affirmative Action purposes, but there is a solid
EEO reason for doing so. They help employers spot
patterns that may indicate questionable behavior. You
don't want to wait for a discrimination lawsuit or a
federal audit before getting a detailed analysis of your
hiring, promotion, and disciplinary practices.

Establish an applicant tracking system that can follow the progress of each applicant through each stage of the process. Conduct adverse impact analyses so you can zero in on potential problems. [Consult your attorney regarding the confidentiality of such studies.] As noted earlier, the best EEO programs are proactive. Your job is to root out the possible - and prevent the actual - discrimination.

Applicant tracking information also gives you a view of the availability of various groups that is far more accurate than the estimates obtained from census statistics. Getting and maintaining that information is one of the most important things the EEO Office (or the HR Department) does.

Get a Clear Definition of an Applicant. It is going to be difficult to have a serious applicant tracking system if anyone who wanders near your office is defined as an applicant. Is someone who sent in an unsolicited resume for a closed recruitment an applicant? Is a person who sent in a letter expressing interest but who did not complete an application form to be considered an applicant? These and other questions need to be sorted out. I favor the rigid approach. I want everyone to have to complete an application form (so we get the same type of information on each applicant) and if a form is not filled out, then the person is not an applicant. Recruitment periods open and close in a reasonable amount of time and only the applications that are received in that period will be considered. No exceptions. It may be brutal but it simplifies things.

Don't Feel That You Have to Consider Everyone Who Applies. Having just said that only those who apply in the recruitment period will be considered, let me make an exception. In a tough economy, you may be swamped with applications; so many in fact that giving them the attention they deserve would take too much time. Here's an alternative: Randomly select a smaller pool from the total one and then carefully analyze those applicants. It makes sense and, provided the screening was indeed random, poses no EEO problems.

Let the Departments Answer for Their Employment Decisions. Don't fall into the trap of having to explain employment decisions that you didn't make. Here's how this happens. Your office monitors Affirmative Action and reports to upper management on the organization's progress. You may advise departments on hiring decisions but, in most cases – a pre-hire monitoring exception is noted below- it is their call, not yours. If a department does a poor job of meeting Affirmative Action goals, why should you be raked over the coals? Let that department director explain to upper management why no women or minorities were interviewed when there were some impressive female and minority candidates in the applicant pool.

Use Pre-Hire Monitoring. Let's say there is a pattern of women or minorities not being hired for certain jobs in a particular department. There may be good, nondiscriminatory reasons why they aren't being hired, but all you know is it's not happening. Your analysis concludes that, given the availability of women or minorities, one would reasonably expect that department would employ more of them. If you simply monitor the results of the department's hiring over the year, by the time you see the bad numbers it will be too late to do anything. The game is over. The jobs have already been filled. It makes sense to require – as part of the Affirmative Action Plan - that the department run its proposed hiring decisions for those jobs by your office before a job offer is made. If their explanation for the selection decision is sound, then they may proceed. If not, then you can try to persuade them to consider other candidates. If the EEO Office and the department cannot reach agreement, then the decision can be appealed to a higher level in the organization, perhaps to the CEO. Pre-hire monitoring gives you significant influence at an important stage of the selection process.

Beware of Rigid Eligible Lists. Employers who rank applicants after the earlier screening process and then put them in rank order on a list are in dangerous territory if they require the hiring departments to interview applicants in the order in which they appeared on the list. Why? Because the screening process may have been discriminatory and so the women and minorities may be lower down on the list. Let's set that aside. Pretend that there is no chance of a disparate impact challenge to the screening process and mechanisms that produced that list. Permit common sense to enter the room. The administrative assistant applicant who scored 88 points in your screening system may have specific experience working for an engineering firm. Your Engineering Department is looking for an administrative assistant. Rather than having to interview a bunch of people with higher scores but less relevant experience, they might want to see if that person with direct experience is the best person for the job. If you permit – as you should – departments to interview anyone who happens to be on the eligible list, they can do so. That makes sense to me provided you follow the rule in the next paragraph.

Don't Abandon the Concept of "Best Qualified."
Always hire the best qualified person. Regard an
eligible list as a list of people who are "in the ballpark"
when it comes to being qualified but don't fall prey to
assuming that they are all equally qualified. Once that
happens, you'll be on the path to justifying hiring
quotas. The hiring department has to determine who
should be interviewed and who the best qualified
person for the specific job is. No winks. No nudges.
Hire the best qualified person.

**Be Careful When Linking Pay to Affirmative
Action Progress**. I've worked in systems where this
was done. The virtue is it gets the attention of
managers. The risk is that it may indirectly encourage
hiring quotas. If you use such links, emphasize that the
grade will be based on good faith efforts and that
quotas are unacceptable.

EEO INVESTIGATIONS

*"Just because nobody complains doesn't mean
all parachutes are perfect."*
- *Benny Hill*

Since discrimination cases can be enormously divisive
and expensive, it is important to have a coherent
approach; a philosophy if you will. Here are some key
components:

Don't Be Taken In By Your Own P.R. The
Black/Hispanic/Gay/Disabled Rights community
group that gave your CEO a nice plaque at its annual
dinner may have done so for a simple reason: Your
organization wrote them a nice fat check. It doesn't
mean that your EEO house is in order. It also doesn't
mean that their undying support is in your pocket.

Know the Management Practices that Spark Cases.
Many, if not most, discrimination cases are not really
caused by discrimination. They are the result of poor
management and/or lousy communication. Your
credibility can increase if you also note changes in
management practices that could reduce the odds of
getting discrimination complaints. The best EEO
Officers know the ins and outs of good management.

Too Many Complaints can be a Problem. So Can Too Few. If your organization rarely gets a discrimination complaint, people may just love working there (hey, it happens) or the complaints may have been driven underground. You want to make it easy for people to file complaints. If your employee grievance and EEO complaint procedures are so narrowly defined that employee problems fall between the cracks, that gap should be addressed. It is not unusual for people to file complaints with the EEOC because they had no other avenue of redress.

Complaints are opportunities to make things better.

"Zero Tolerance" is Brain-Dead. Don't have zero tolerance policies on discrimination and harassment. (I mention harassment specifically because harassment policies are noted for "zero tolerance" language.)

Zero tolerance is a mechanical and mindless approach. It removes thought from a process that requires a lot of thought and, one would hope, some compassion. It can put you in the position of having to be harsher than the facts would warrant or backing off and making a mockery of the zero tolerance pronouncements. If you have such policies, get rid of them. Give yourself greater flexibility and more accountability.

Update Your Disciplinary Policies and Procedures. A policy or procedure gets added today. Some more are added two years later. A few more revisions are then made and, as time takes its toll, you have inconsistent disciplinary policies. Attorneys who seek to poke holes in disciplinary cases will start to salivate when they see any conflicts. Catch and correct the problems beforehand by having periodic reviews by your attorney.

Know the Scope of Your Investigations. There are certain issues, such as criminal matters, that you don't want to touch. The appropriate law enforcement agency should be handling a criminal case. The labor relations office gets the union matters and the employee relations people may get run-of-the-mill bad management issues. Your territory is discrimination. Be very wary of leaving it. You risk taking on more work than is wise and getting outside of your area of expertise. You may also be walking on someone else's turf.

Have a Clear and Credible Internal Complaint Procedure. In order to have a credible internal discrimination complaint investigation process these elements must be present: The process must be Prompt, Thorough, and Objective and appropriate action must be taken based upon the findings. The complaint procedure should be easy to understand and it should be posted. I suggest sending it to the employees once a year with their paychecks or separately to them if they have direct deposit.

Don't Tell Employees to Take Discrimination Complaints to Their Supervisors. I've seen some complaint procedures that give the employee the option of bringing the problem to the attention of the immediate supervisor. That is a very bad move. It makes the complaint process as strong as the weakest supervisor. As a result, if a supervisor hears about a discrimination complaint then dawdles about and does not take appropriate action, management has been informed and, via its supervisor, done nothing. That does not look good in court. In fairness to supervisors, we should acknowledge that not all complaints are worded in the most articulate manner and they may be quickly mentioned in the course of business. Let your policy be crystal clear: All discrimination complaints should go to the EEO Office.

Beware of Fatigue. You don't want investigations to drag on but you also don't want to exhaust your investigator. A tired investigator is one who will make mistakes. Make sure that the person is getting sufficient rest.

Report Bad News Immediately. The EEO Officer should keep the Chief Executive Officer briefed on the status of any discrimination complaints. Don't sit on that news until it is time for your monthly report.

Establish Your Ability to Gain Access to Documents and Witnesses. If your office is going to investigate discrimination complaints, it will have to be able to check HR files and department files and line up witnesses without undue delay or inference from the departments. That ability needs to be firmly established. If the process is too complicated, you may be tempted to bypass a source of evidence that ultimately may turn out to be vital.

Don't Set a Deadline for Discrimination Investigations. If your regulation states that all discrimination investigations must be completed in two weeks, you're screwed if you get a complex investigation or key witnesses are out on leave. Setting a deadline is one of the worst mistakes you can make.

Distinguish Between Internal Complaints, External Complaints, and Potential Complaints. Internal complaints are discrimination complaints filed with your office. External complaints are filed with outside agencies, such as the federal Equal Employment Opportunity Commission or the state civil rights agency. Potential complaints are trickier. An example of a potential complaint is when an employee comes in and says: "I really haven't been turned down for a promotion yet, but I sense that I'm going to be turned down and that it's going to be because of my race. I want to go on record now as having this concern because if I wait until later someone might just say that I'm just upset for being rejected."

It would be premature to launch an investigation. The person has not been harmed. The selection decision has not been made. But it does make sense for the EEO office professional to write a memo to file on the conversation and tuck it into a potential complaint file. Now it may be argued that the person has just alleged the existence of a hostile work environment, but I've seen cases in which there is no evidence aside from a feeling. You can imagine how you'd look if you confronted a department head about the possible discrimination which has not yet occurred and which is due to reasons the complainant cannot describe.

A virtue of potential complaints is that you may begin to notice a pattern. No one has formally filed a complaint of fire but they are mentioning a lot of smoke. In that case, I'd recommend launching an investigation "on your own motion" so to speak, even though there is not a charging party. That may even occur in the wake of a single potential complaint if there is a reasonable basis to conclude that a problem exists.

Recognize the Avenues of Attack. Here are some of the common ways in which lawyers may challenge your internal EEO investigations: The investigator is biased; the investigator is incompetent; the investigation was not thorough; the investigator lacks the authority to conduct the investigation; due process was violated; the employer's own policy was violated; the findings are improper; the recommendation is inappropriate; and the root cause of the investigation was poisonous.

Be prepared to close all of those avenues.

Review All Findings Before They Are Finalized. Never, ever, let your investigator complete an investigation until it has been reviewed by you.

Keep Tabs on the Cost of The Potential Complaints That Are Resolved. Include the potential complaints in your calculations because often they are The Case That Didn't Happen. You may have made a phone call or, through discussion with the employee, found that the problem could be resolved through other channels. Your office should get credit for those actions because, in many cases, if that action had not been taken then a case would have been filed.

It can help at performance review time to calculate the amount of staff time, both within and without your office, which was saved by actions that resolved potential complaints before they became real complaints. Your team deserves credit for saving time and money.

Red-Flag Relevant Personnel Files. If a personnel file may be relevant to an EEO case, you don't want to find that it has been destroyed. Red-flag such files and make it clear that your office should be consulted before the file is deleted or destroyed.

Keep Complaint Files Separate from Personnel Files. The employee's personnel file should contain no mention of any discrimination complaints. You don't want to abet retaliation.

Get Specific Allegations in Writing. The specific allegations in any discrimination complaint should be in writing. This helps to clarify the issues. It also thwarts a losing charging party's later efforts to claim that another matter had been alleged.

—

Any External Discrimination Complaints Should Go Directly to Your Office. You don't want an external complaint to sit on some department director's desk for three weeks before you're brought into the picture. Make sure that the outside enforcement agencies know where to send the complaints and that your department heads know to send them on if, for any reason, they receive a complaint.

Don't Let Departments Conduct Their Own Investigations. All discrimination investigations should be handled by your office. The departments may want to do their own investigations, but there is too high a risk of cover-up. This is a particular problem in the public sector where police departments often want to be an entity unto themselves. They'll note that they have a highly trained Internal Affairs Bureau and that they should be permitted to let IA conduct the investigation. Don't let them do it. If you do, you will have lost control of one of the most high-profile targets for discrimination complaints and will have established a terrible precedent. [One of the lines I've heard is that cops won't talk to non-cops. That is a hoot. I never had a problem getting cops to talk. The greater problem was getting them to shut up. Police and Fire departments are notorious gossip mills.] The EEO Office should have a monopoly on EEO investigations.

Move Cautiously on Administrative Suspensions.
Some organizations rush to put employees on
administrative leave if they are the subject of an
internal investigation. This is wise if there is a serious
risk of either harm or the appearance of harm should
the person remain on the job. In most cases, putting
the employee on administrative leave is a questionable
practice for several reasons. First, it is costly. You are
paying them to sit at home. Second, it raises the profile
of the case and fuels rumors at work. Finally, why
have the employee fuming at home and thumbing
through the Attorneys section of the Yellow Pages
when they could be at work?

Beware of When Internal Complaints Go External.
If you close internal complaints whenever the person
also files with an external enforcement agency such as
the U.S. Equal Employment Opportunity Commission,
that action may be deemed retaliation. This poses a
real problem. At one point you've been objectively
investigating an internal complaint against one of your
departments and the next you are expected to advise
that same department when it responds to the
employee's external complaint. Some EEO offices
hold the internal complaint in abeyance while
responding to the external one, knowing that the
outcome of their review of the merits of the external
complaint will ultimately affect how they proceed on
the internal one. This can be further complicated when
the complaints raise somewhat different issues. It is
wise to discuss the matter with your organization's
attorney in order to make sure that your course of
action has the attorney's support.

Watch Out for Group Problems that Are Hidden in Individual Complaints. I have some scars to show in this subject. What happens is Jill files a discrimination complaint against Jack. As you get into the investigation, you find that various factions line up to support either Jack or Jill. You also discover something else: Jack and Jill are both pretty good employees but when the two are in the same room, the worst aspects of their personalities emerge. Each is guilty of failing to work with the other in a positive manner. If you could wave a wand, you'd turn both of them into toads and then set fire to the swamp. The problem is your marching orders are to find out if Jack is guilty of what Jill has alleged. Now is a very good time to get with the best employment attorney you can find and work out a plan of action. The organization is trying to fix a group problem with an individual solution.

Have the Courage to Use Common Sense. That earlier scenario brings up an especially interesting subject. EEO investigations are usually conducted with an eye on the potential for an EEO lawsuit. The investigators and the lawyers all have on their law hats and, truth be known, the opposing parties are probably checking out their hats in the mirror. What does not receive sufficient attention – possibly because lawyers are the high priests of our society and their utterances have almost religious weight – is the management component. It is possible that the emphasis on the legal side may produce grave damage on the management side.

Let me give an example. I once encountered a highly accomplished female executive who had mentioned to her employer that one of her peers occasionally made comments that were sexually inappropriate. The comments were not extreme, but were simply in poor taste. They certainly didn't bother this woman because she was sophisticated and strong enough to have diced up the man before breakfast. She passed along the information with a warning: If the employer launched an investigation based on her reporting of the comments, she'd resign. She wanted the matter handled discreetly, not with a sledge hammer.

Some employers (and many attorneys) would say, "Too bad. Once we learn of any potential harassment, we have to launch a thorough investigation."

To which I reply, "Launching a mega-investigation in this situation makes no sense. All you would accomplish would be to embarrass the man and get the resignation of the woman."

What I recommended, of course, was to have an "investigation" that was not a full-fledged version but which was more of an "audit." Recommendations were made, the word about language was discreetly passed, and the problem was solved with no embarrassment and no resignations.

You have to use common sense.

Beware of Nuisance Settlements. If your employer gains a reputation as an easy settlement employer, you can expect to see a lot of letters from lawyers. Be very cautious when deciding to settle cases that are clearly without merit. You don't want supervisors to feel that they've been sold out by upper management. To maintain credibility, you need to settle the cases that have merit and fight the ones that are worthless.

Avoid Alibi Creation Games. "Alibi Creation" is what I call Fake Action. In other words, you don't directly address a problem, you send out a memo. You don't confront the one employee who is a problem in the Widget Department, you hold training for the entire department. Your focus is less on crafting a solution than it is on finding an alibi; some action that will show that you did something, however feeble it may be.

If They Bring a Dog, You Bring a Dog. If the other side is going to have a lawyer in the room, make sure that you have a lawyer in the room and don't bring a Chihuahua if they have a Doberman.

DIVERSITY MANAGEMENT STRATEGIES

"The other day I got out my can-opener and was opening a can of worms when I thought, 'What am I doing?'"
- *Jack Handey*

Diversity is Not a Magic Solution. There are times when I hear diversity enthusiasts speaking and I wonder at their ability to ignore the hard lessons of human experience. In their gospel, the magic talisman of Diversity need only to be invoked to create a team that will…well, this new team will just be fantastic because we'll have all of these diverse groups together and they will respect and love one another and they'll be on the same page and, just watch, it will be sooo great.

Kumbaya, baby.

Let's get something straight. Diversity is not a magic formula for great performance. [Despite their recent problems, Toyota functioned quite well for years without an ethnically diverse management team and I doubt if women are packing their top ranks.] Diversity can be beneficial, but it can be also be divisive.

Take a look at the carnage of Beirut and Bosnia. The diverse groups in those spots have been at each other's throats for years. Unfortunately, a quick tour of the world will reveal that they are not rare exceptions. Diversity does not produce an inherent advantage. When groups know one another they do not necessarily love one another.

The multiculturalists who want to toss out the old melting pot theory and replace it with a salad bowl should think again. The melting pot had its flaws - not every group melted at the same rate and the nation won't fall apart if a group wants to have a St. Patrick's Day parade or a Gay Pride Day – but, like democracy, its virtues far outweigh its negatives. One of the unifying concepts of this nation is we're supposed to be Americans first and whatever racial or ethnic identification we possess should be miles behind that status. [The sounds you just heard are thousands of multiculturalists collapsing and drumming the floor with their heels.]

Do you think some people may not like those nationalist overtones? Well, wait until they get a dose of tribalism. They'll realize that nationalism was and remains a pretty forward-thinking concept.

Let's keep stirring that melting pot.

And while I'm on this soapbox: There's a dirty little secret that I seldom hear at diversity confabs or read in diversity publications. Some of the groups that can make your workforce more diverse won't necessarily embrace your equal opportunity program. A person whose religious beliefs reject women and gays in the workplace is not exactly going to fit the image of a happy, jolly, diversity-celebrating co-worker. You'll find no rainbow on that person's car bumper.

That's another reason why EEO trumps Diversity. I don't care if your culture or beliefs say that showing up on time is not necessary or that you shouldn't work alongside women or gays. If you work here, you are going to show up on time and you will work cheerfully and well with women and gays. And if they don't work equally well with you, then we'll gladly address their attitudes.

Equal opportunity is non-negotiable.

That's macro. In order to counter some of the micro-pitfalls that lurk in poorly-managed Diversity Management programs, here are some steps to avoid:

Don't Be a Guilt-Peddler. The Race Card isn't accepted in very many establishments nowadays. This doesn't mean that there aren't valid racial discrimination cases. It is sad to have to note that in the 21st Century, there are still such violations of decency. The bigots shall always be with us, but this isn't the Fifties and the Sixties and people who repeatedly cry "Racist" or "Sexist" or "Homophobe" when the allegation is baseless reduce the stigma of discrimination.

Guilt is a lousy motivator anyway. Scaring people is not as effective as persuading them. Using guilt as leverage for change will only increase resistance.

Get the White Guys on Board. An EEO program will not work if it is only seen as a program for women and minorities. It has to become Everybody's Program. Run far and fast from any diversity programs that mock or place special guilt on white men.

A large portion of the most powerful people in your organization is probably composed of white males. You won't succeed without the support of those white guys and, unless they are complete wimps, you won't gain that support by denouncing them or telling them how privileged they are. [Newsflash: Not every white guy came from a wealthy family where chicken cordon bleu was served on china and the dinner conversation swirled about the latest interview on National Public Radio.].

75

Treat People as Individuals, Not as Group Representatives. Ed has been named to a committee to review promotional practices. Ed happens to be Hispanic, but is he expected to be representative of all Hispanics? Has he magically been designated to speak for the amazingly diverse group conveniently labeled the "Hispanic Community?" [That term takes in groups as different as Cuban Americans and Puerto Ricans. Check out their voting patterns.] He's also over fifty and a veteran. Does that mean he speaks for those groups? And when he speaks, how do we know which group he's speaking for? [Hmm, I think his remarks just slipped from Hispanic into Fluent Old Man.] And when can we tell that we are getting Ed's real opinion rather than the opinion that he thinks he ought to hold as a group member? The solution is simple: Let Ed speak for Ed. Don't pretend that he is speaking for an entire group. If he happens to bring in a perspective that you otherwise would not have had, then fine, but let him bring it as Ed.

Favor Fat Committees. By "fat committees" I don't mean groups for People of Size (great term). I worry about organizations that have separate committees for Blacks, Hispanics, Women, Gays/Lesbians/Transsexuals/Bisexuals, People with Disabilities, Seniors, and, yes, People of Size. My concern stems from this general rule: The narrower the group, the more unreasonable its demands. It helps to have people from various groups serve on the same committees related to hiring standards, promotions, etc., so they can understand that they aren't the only game in town. They can see other groups have concerns that may not neatly mesh with their own.

It is also much easier to provide staff support to one committee than for seven or more.

Speak Truth to the Advocacy Groups. Never lie to the advocacy groups. Never feed them a line. The best example I've seen of an executive meeting with an advocacy group was years ago when the head of the Phoenix Transit Department met with what was then called the Mayor's Committee on Employment of the Handicapped. I was the Mayor's Liaison to that committee which had people from a variety of disability-related groups. There were blind people, deaf people, people who used wheelchairs, and several other group representatives. Their militancy ranged from mild to strong.

They'd received advance notice that the Public Transit Director would talk to them about bus service and so they were loaded for bear. The bitter joke was that Phoenix had a solar bus system because the buses stopped running after dark.

I introduced the Director and he immediately began asking the committee members what they wanted from the City when it came to public transit. As the ideas flew, he wrote them on a flip chart. He soon had a long list.

At that point, the suggestions/demands ceased and he had, to my mind, his finest moment. He turned to the group and said, "I can give you everything that you've asked for. Just give me the money."

The room was silent and then, one-by-one, the grins started to appear. People who'd been barking at me for months about the lousy bus service were smiling. The reason soon became apparent:

They knew he was telling them the truth.

They knew that if the City Council gave him the money for these programs, he could do exactly what they wanted, but they also knew that the City Council was not going to do that.

It was Reality TV before Reality TV.

Keep that in mind when meeting with groups. Be frank. Don't say anything that will be embarrassing, but be frank.

Quick tip: As an EEO Officer, I got into the habit of giving my home phone number to the leaders of various interest groups. I invited them to call me at home if they ever needed to reach me on a weekend. I scored a lot of points with the gesture and never got a call.

SUMMARY

I've taken some shots at EEO offices and professionals in this book, but they were taken for one reason only: I care.

An organization and a society that pays close attention to providing equal opportunity is going to be far more competitive than ones that do not. People sometimes wonder why the United States is such a productive nation. Here's one factor: We don't rule out large portions of our talent base.

Look at many other nations. You have the wrong religion or are of the wrong race? Forget it. You're a woman? Go home. You have a disability? They don't even want to look at you. You are old? Go sit on a porch. You are gay? Well, in some places you are fortunate if you survive that answer.

The United States strives to get more and more talent into the workplace while many of its competitors bar massive numbers of highly capable people.

EEO is too important to be done poorly. If you care about it, you'll want it to be handled as competently as possible. You'll get angry at the charlatans who use it as a shake-down device. You'll bristle at condescension and tokenism. You'll want to see serious efforts and you won't accept window dressing.

If this is your attitude, good for you. We are allies in one of the most important campaigns ever to reach the workplace: the campaign to tap the great potential of the individual.

Let's get to work.

RECOMMENDED READING

Russell L. Ackoff and Sheldon Rovin, *Beating the System: Using Creativity to Outsmart Bureaucracies*. [San Francisco: Berrett-Koehler Publishers, Inc., 2005.]

David Bernstein, *You Can't Say That!: The Growing Threat to Civil Liberties from Antidiscrimination Laws*. [Washington, D.C.: Cato Institute, 2003.]

Richard Bernstein, *Dictatorship of Virtue: How the Battle over Multiculturalism is Reshaping Our Schools, Our Country, Our Lives*. [New York: Vintage Books, 1995.]

Stephen M.R. Covey, *The Speed of Trust: The One Thing That Changes Everything*. [New York: Free Press, 2006.]

Amitai Etzioni, *The Spirit of Community: The Reinvention of American Society*. [New York: Simon & Schuster, 1993.]

Richard Farson and Ralph Keyes, *Whoever Makes the Most Mistakes Wins: The Paradox of Innovation*. [New York: The Free Press, 2002.]

David W. Hutton, *The Change Agent's Handbook: A Survival Guide for Quality Improvement Champions*. [Milwaukee: ASQC Press, 1994.]

Bruce A. Jacobs, *Race Manners: Navigating the Minefield between Black and White Americans.* [New York: Arcade Publishing, 1999.]

Edward E. Lawler III, *Talent: Making People Your Competitive Advantage.* [San Francisco: Jossey-Bass, 2008.]

Glenn C. Loury, *One By One From the Inside Out: Essays and Reviews on Race and Responsibility in America.* [New York: The Free Press, 1995.]

David H. Maister, Charles H. Green, and Robert M. Galford, *The Trusted Advisor.* [New York: The Free Press, 2000.]

Walter K. Olson, *The Excuse Factory: How Employment Law is Paralyzing the American Workplace.* [New York: The Free Press, 1997.]

David Osborne and Peter Plastrik, *Banishing Bureaucracy: The Five Strategies for Reinventing Government.* [New York: Addison-Wesley Publishing Company, Inc., 1997.]

Clotaire Rapaille, *The Culture Code.* [New York: Broadway Books, 2006.]

Thomas Sowell, *Ethnic America.* [New York: Basic Books, 1981.]

Thomas Sowell, *Civil Rights: Rhetoric or Reality?* [New York: William Morrow and Company, 1984.]

Shelby Steele, *The Content of Our Character: A New Vision of Race in America*. [New York: St. Martin's Press, 1992.]

Shelby Steele, *White Guilt: How Blacks and Whites Destroyed the Promise of the Civil Rights Era*. [New York: Harper Perennial, 2007.]

Charles J. Sykes, *A Nation of Victims: The Decay of the American Character*. [New York: St. Martin's Press, 1992.]

Stephan and Abigail Thernstrom, *American in Black and White: One Nation, Indivisible*. [New York; Simon & Schuster, 1999.]

Michael Wade, *All I Said Was...What Every Supervisor, Employee, and Team Should Know to Avoid Insults, Lawsuits, and the Six O'Clock News*. [Amazon: CreateSpace, 2010.]

Michael Wade, *How to Make Presentations to Councils and Boards*. [Amazon: CreateSpace, 2010.]

Steven L. Willborn, Stewart J. Schwab, John F. Burton, Jr., and Gillian L.L. Lester, *Employment Law: Cases and Materials*. [Newark: Lexus Nexus, 2007.]

James Q. Wilson, *Bureaucracy: What Government Agencies Do and Why They Do It*. [New York: Basic Boos, 1989.]

Tom Wolfe, *Radical Chic and Mau-Mauing the Flak Catchers*. [New York: Farrar, Straus and Giroux, 1970.]

About the Author

Michael Wade is a partner with Sanders Wade Rodarte Consulting Inc. in Phoenix, Arizona. Prior to starting his consulting practice, Michael served as the EEO Administrator for the City of Phoenix and as the Command Equal Opportunity Officer for the United States Army Criminal Investigation Command in Washington, D.C. He has advised corporate executives, police and fire chiefs, city managers, Army generals, professional athletes, and entry-level employees on sensitive issues. His blog – Execupundit.com- has an international readership. Michael holds a Juris Doctorate from the University of Arizona College of Law and is a graduate of the Defense Equal Opportunity Management Institute in Florida. He is the author of "Leadership's Adversary: Winning the War between Leadership and Management"; "How to Make Presentations to Councils and Boards"; "All I Said Was…What Every Supervisor, Employee, and Team Should Know to Avoid Insults, Lawsuits, and the Six O'Clock News"; and "The Bitter Issue: The Right to Work Law in Arizona." For information on Michael's training and coaching services or to get on his e-newsletter list, email him at michael@swrci.com or call 602-788-1717.